Alaska Animals -

Where Do They Go At 40 Below?

by
Bernd and Susan Richter

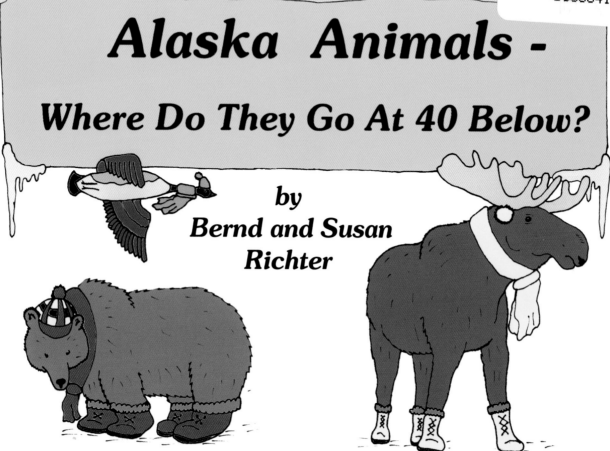

Published by
Saddle Pal Creations, Inc., Wasilla, Alaska, USA

Acknowledgements:
We owe special thanks to Linda Thurston and Bernice Sheldon for their
editing efforts and suggestions.

To the memory of Reuben Eaton III,
who made us smile even at 40 below.

More children's books by Bernd and Susan Richter available from Saddle Pal Creations, Inc.:

* *When Grandma and Grandpa visited Alaska they ...*
* *Grandma and Grandpa visit Denali Natl. Park*
* *Grandma and Grandpa Cruise Alaska's Inside Passage*
* *Grandma and Grandpa Ride the Alaska Train*
* *When G'ma and G'pa rode the Alaska Train (board b.)*
* *When G'ma and G'pa rode the White Pass (board b.)*
* *When G'ma and G'pa Cruised through Alaska (board b.)*
* *When Grandma visited Alaska she ...*
* *The Little Bear Who Didn't Want to Hibernate*
* *Good Morning Alaska - Good Morning Little Bear*
* *Alaskan Toys - For Girls and Boys*
* *Goodnight Alaska - Goodnight Little Bear (board book)*
* *Peek-A-Boo Alaska (lift-the-flap board book)*
* *How Animal Moms Love Their Babies (board book)*
* *Touch and Feel Alaska's Animals (board book)*

* *How Alaska Got Its Flag*
* *There Was A Little Bear*
* *There Was A Little Porcupine*
* *I See You Through My Heart*
* *Do Alaskans Live in Igloos?*
* *Cruising Alaska's Inside Passage*
* *Listen to Alaska's Animals (sound book)*
* *She's My Mommy Too!*
* *My Alaska Animals - Can You name Them?*
* *The Twelve Days of Christmas in Alaska*
* *Discover Alaska's Denali park*
* *Uncover Alaska's Wonders (a lift-the-flap book)*
* *Grandma and Grandpa Love Their RV*
* *Old Maid - Alaska Style (card game)*
* *A Bus Ride Into Denali (board book).... and more*

Look at these books by visiting our website **www.alaskachildrensbooks.com**

Introduction

Alaska is famous for being one of the last true wilderness areas remaining in North America. Here, wild animals still have plenty of room to live a free life. But there is something else for which Alaska is famous. It is known as the land of snow, ice, and long, cold winters. Temperatures sometimes drop to 40 or more degrees below zero, and when the wind blows, wind-chill factors can go to minus 100 degrees Fahrenheit. Look at this thermo-meter and find minus 40 degrees. Then find out what your out-side temperature is right now. Most likely, there will be a big difference. At such extreme temperatures, exposed skin, especially on ears, noses, and fingers, can freeze within minutes. Therefore, when it is that cold, people and their pets go inside and huddle around warm stoves. Alaska's wild animals don't have heated houses. Where do they go at 40 below? Continue reading, and you will find out.

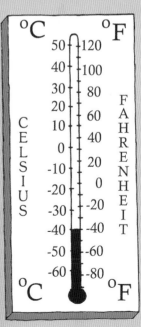

How to use this book:
- *Bold text for ages 3 to 7; bonus text for ages 5 to 10*
- *Green text pages = Summer*
- *Blue text pages = Winter*

"Whales in the Summer"

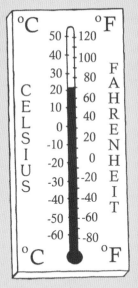

Young Readers:

Whales are the largest animals in the entire world. They live in the oceans. Whales eat their food under water, but they have to come to the surface to breathe air. In the winter, a thick layer of ice covers much of the ocean surface surrounding Alaska. How can the whales breathe then? Where can the whales go to breathe?

Advanced Readers:

The blue whale is the largest of all whales. It grows up to 100 feet long and weighs more than 100 tons. At that size and weight, it is no surprise that the world's largest animal has to live in the water. The blue whale would be crushed by its own weight if it lived on land. Even though whales live in water, they aren't fish but mammals. They breathe oxygen like you and me. Of course, whales can hold their breath much longer than we can. They usually come to the surface for breathing every 5 to 15 minutes, but some can dive up to 1 hour. When they finally exhale at the surface, you can see a spray of air and water coming out of their blowholes. Ocean water doesn't freeze as easily as river water because of its high salt content. Still, it gets so cold in Alaska that a thick ice layer forms on most of the ocean surface. Only ships known as ice breakers can make it through the sea ice then. What does that mean for the whales? Where do they go at 40 below?

"Whales in the Winter"

Young Readers:

In the winter, most whales swim far away from Alaska to the south where the waters are much warmer. While they are living in the warmer seas, mother whales give birth to little baby whales. By the time winter is over, the baby whales are big enough to swim with their moms to Alaska, where there is plenty of food for them to eat.

Advanced Readers:

Their travel back and forth, spending part of the year in one area and the rest of the year in another far-away area, is called "migration." Some of the whales, such as the gray and the blue whales, go to calving grounds along the coasts of California and Mexico. Others, such as the humpback whale, may go there or to Pacific ocean islands, such as Hawaii. This is also where the sperm whale goes. One of the few whales that stays in arctic waters all year long is the bowhead whale. The bowhead spends its summers north of Alaska in the Beaufort Sea and its winters west of Alaska in the Bering Sea, even though sea ice covers large parts of the ocean. In the Beaufort Sea, there is sea ice even in the summer. So, how can the bowhead breathe?

To get to air, the bowhead uses a special weapon. On the top of its huge head is a large bony shield, which allows the whale to break a hole into the ice as long as it isn't thicker than 1.5 feet. The shield protects the whale's brain, while its enormous body size of up to 60 feet and huge weight of up to 100 tons supplies the power. It is believed that the bowhead sends out sonar waves to determine the location and thickness of ice, as well as the location of any cracks in the ice surface.

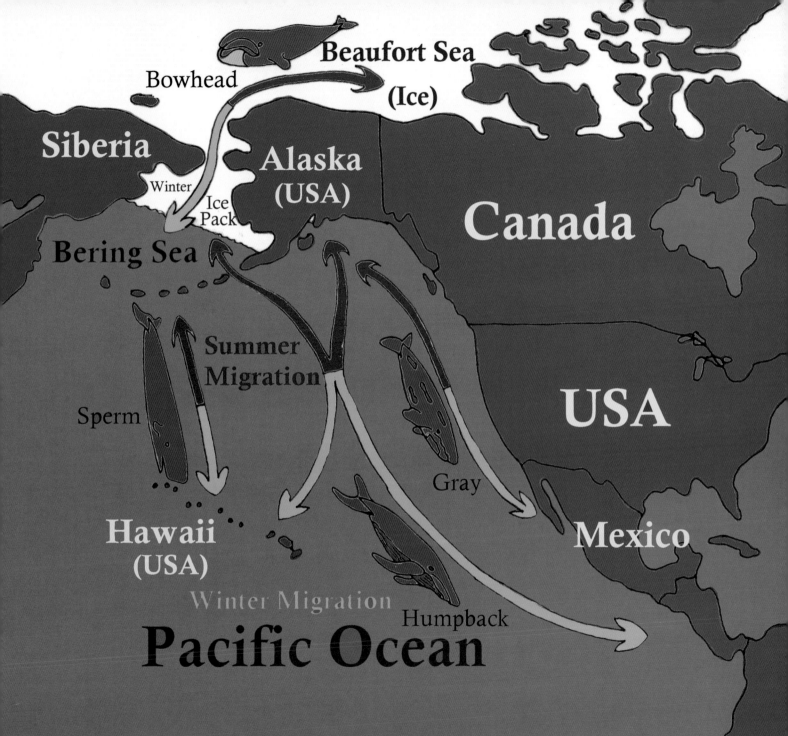

"Moose in the Summer"

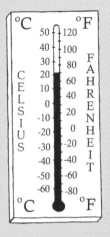

Young Readers:

There is an animal in Alaska that looks similar to a horse. But you cannot ride it because it is too wild. It is called a "moose." In the summer, they like to eat fresh leaves from bushes and trees. Sometimes, they walk out into small lakes to eat fresh, green plants that grow on the lake bottom. In the winter, a thick layer of ice covers the lakes and there aren't any leaves left on the bushes. Where can the moose go to find food then? Moose can swim, but they can't swim as fast or as far as whales do. Where do the moose go at 40 below?

Advanced Readers:

Moose are the largest members of the deer family in North America, standing 6 to 7 feet tall at the shoulder and weighing up to 1,700 pounds. They are definitely bigger than horses. The male moose (bull) can be easily distinguished from the female (cow) because only the bulls grow antlers. These antlers can grow up to 6 feet across and then fall off at the end of each year only to grow back even bigger the next year. The biggest antler usually identifies the lead bull within a territory. In the summer, the moose diet consists mainly of aquatic plants and leaves and buds from bushes and trees. They don't grow in the winter, which is quite a dilemma for the moose. What do they eat then? Where do they go at 40 below?

"Moose in the Winter"

Young Readers:

Moose spend winters in pretty much the same areas that they spend their summers. Their thick fur keeps them nice and warm, and their long legs allow them to walk through deep snow. Their fur is so thick that moose can even sleep comfortably on the snow. As for food, they simply change what they eat. In the winter, moose almost exclusively eat twigs of bushes and bark of trees that aren't covered by the snow.

Advanced Readers:

Winters can be very tough on moose, especially when there is heavy snow-fall. The more snow, the less brush stays uncovered for them to eat. If the winter is also a long one, moose may run out of food before the winter is over. It is not uncommon in Alaska for moose to be starving by the end of winter. That is why it is so important for them to put on as much weight as possible during the summer - the fatter the better. This is one of nature's ways to make sure that only the strongest animals survive.

Other examples of animals that do not migrate but stay in the same areas are the wolf, musk ox, fox, Dall sheep, and mountain goat.

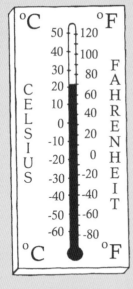

"Ptarmigan in the Summer"

Young Readers:

In 1955, schoolchildren in Alaska were asked which bird they would like to see as the official state bird of Alaska. Do you know the state bird of your state or country? The Alaska schoolchildren chose the ptarmigan as the state bird. Can you find this bird on the picture to the right?

Advanced Readers:

There are three different types of ptarmigan in Alaska. The willow ptarmigan live mainly on the tundra - wide open areas with only few trees. The other two, the white-tailed ptarmigan and the rock ptarmigan, live among the rocks in the barren and rugged mountain areas. The one shown here is the rock ptarmigan. Its feathers, called plumage, are colored like the surrounding rocks, which is perfect for hiding from enemies. Blending in with the surroundings is called "camouflage." But what happens in the winter when everything is white and covered with snow? How and where can the ptarmigan hide then? Where do they go at 40 below?

"Ptarmigan in the Winter"

Young Readers:

Where is the ptarmigan? Did it migrate like the whale? No, it stayed in Alaska. And it is in this picture. In fact, there are two of them! They are hard to find because they have changed their color. When winter arrives, ptarmigan slowly lose their dark feathers and grow white ones in their place. By the time the land is covered with snow, the ptarmigan turn completely white, with the exception of their beaks and eyes.

Advanced Readers:

The ptarmigan put on their winter camouflage to hide them from predators. For protection against the cold, ptarmigan have two layers of feathers. The outer layer consists of tough feathers that keep out wind and water. The inner layer consists of fluffy soft feathers that keep their warm body heat in. When it gets bitter cold, though, the ptarmigan burrow down into the snow where it is warmer than at the surface. During the winter, there is less for them to eat than in the summer because there aren't any insects, leaves, or flowers around. But they do just fine on a diet of twigs and buds from bushes. Some other animals that change their color to white in the winter are the snowshoe hare, the arctic fox, and the weasel.

"Caribou in the Summer"

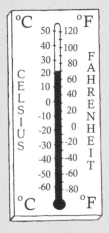

Young Readers:

In Alaska, there are more caribou than people. Most of the time, caribou live together as families of 10 to 20 animals. But sometimes, many, many families come together to form herds of thousands and thousands of caribou. When so many animals come together, they need plenty of leaves and grasses to be available for all of them to eat. In the winter, there are no leaves on bushes and the grasses are covered by snow. What do the caribou eat then? Will they eat twigs, branches, and bark like the moose do?

Advanced Readers:

The term "band" is used when talking about a small group of caribou. Up to three times a year, in the spring, in early summer, and then again in late fall, scattered bands come together to form huge herds that migrate all over Alaska and Canada in search of calving grounds and feeding areas. Caribou live on the tundra, which they like for several reasons. For one, the tundra provides nourishment in the form of grasses, leaves, and dry, crust-like growth called lichens. Second, because of the lack of trees or high brush, predators, such as wolves and bears, can't sneak up on them. Third, there often is a nice breeze that helps keep the pesky mosquitoes away. Sometimes in the spring, caribou migrate to the mountains where it is too cold for mosquitoes. But how do they find food when there is a thick layer of snow over the entire country? Where do the caribou go at 40 below?

"Caribou in the Winter"

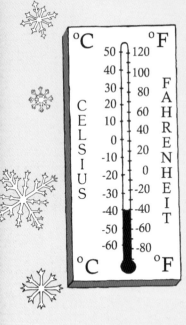

Young Readers:

Caribou don't mind when winter comes. They have an especially thick fur coat that keeps the warmth in and the cold out. And for food, they walk to areas where the snow cover is the thinnest. These are usually treeless and high-lying areas where strong winds blow fresh snow away. The caribou use their strong hooves to paw the snow away to get to edible plants.

Advanced Readers:

When winter arrives, caribou finally get relief from one of their worst enemies - the mosquitoes. During the summer, mosquitoes drive the poor caribou almost insane, biting them in such great numbers that they lose up to one pint of blood per day. That is why caribou sometimes go to snow fields in the middle of the summer to get away from the pesky mosquitoes. Obviously, the cold isn't much of a problem for the caribou because their fur is made of special hair. Each hair is hollow and shaped like a tiny baseball bat with the thick part at the end. Both of these features create an insulating air layer that keeps heat inside. Availability of food is a problem in the winter, though. That is why caribou migrate long distances to new feeding grounds, which can be as far away as Canada.

"Canada Geese in the Summer"

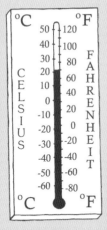

Young Readers:

There are just as many Canada geese in Alaska as there are caribou. In contrast to most other animals, the Canada geese don't mind if people live close by. Geese like to nest in open meadows, even if it is in the middle of town, as long as there is plenty of food for them. Actually, if the meadow is in the middle of town, there may be even more food because some people like to feed the pretty Canada geese. In the winter, their meadows are blanketed by snow. Where do the geese rest and what do they eat then?

Advanced Readers:

In addition to the availability of abundant food, Canada geese prefer to live on open meadows because there is maximum protection from predators. The more open an area, the more difficult it is for a predator to sneak up on them. This way, the geese have a good chance to fly away from any threat. But they don't always fly away, especially during breeding season. Geese can be very aggressive and don't hesitate to attack humans if disturbed by them. Still, what can the geese do against the snow and the bitter cold? Could they possibly huddle together in caves to stay warm like bats do? Where do you think the geese go at 40 below?

"Canada Geese in the Winter"

°C   °F

50   120
40   100
30   80
20   60
10   40
0   20
-10   0
-20   -20
-30   -40
-40
-50   -60
-60   -80

CELSIUS

FAHRENHEIT

°C   °F

Young Readers:

Canada geese are very smart. When they feel winter coming, almost all of them leave Alaska for warmer weather, just as the whales do. The only difference is that the geese fly instead of swim. Some geese will fly 5,000 miles or more to reach their wintering grounds. Canada geese fly south in large groups and in a flight formation that looks like the letter "V." When Alaskans see the geese fly south, they know that winter will be here soon. And when the geese return again the next year, it is a clear sign that the long winter is over and spring is here at last. In areas where there aren't any geese, it is the arrival of another bird, the robin, that marks the beginning of spring.

Advanced Readers:

Only in southeastern Alaska where winters are milder and shorter than in the rest of the state is there a species of Canada geese that doesn't fly south for the winter. These geese have adapted to the cool climate. Most other bird species live in Alaska only part of the year and migrate in winter. Of the migrating birds, the arctic tern flies the farthest, traveling all the way to Antarctica, some 10,000 miles away from Alaska.

"Fish in the Summer"

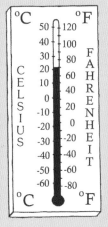

Young Readers:

If you think there are so many caribou and geese in Alaska, you should see the number of fish. In the summer, millions and millions of fish swim in Alaska's rivers and lakes. Sometimes, there are so many fish you can almost walk into the river and pick them up by hand. But that is not allowed. To catch a fish, a fisherman must use a fishing rod or a net. In the winter, it is so cold in Alaska that rivers may freeze all the way to the bottom. Where can the fish swim then?

Advanced Readers:

Alaska is famous for its huge salmon runs. Different salmon species return from the ocean to their birthplace in freshwater streams, lakes and rivers to spawn. The runs occur at different times throughout the year, which makes for a long fishing season. Salmon make up a large share of Alaska's fishing industry, which is the biggest in the United States. Huge fishing boats catch salmon miles out in the ocean. Closer to shore, smaller fishing boats take their share of the catch. Of the fish that come into the rivers, sport fishermen and subsistence users take their limit. Even though many fish are caught each year, plenty of them remain due to fishing limits that allow enough fish to return to their spawning grounds. Of these, each female salmon will lay 2,000 to 15,000 eggs. She deposits them in nests called redds which she digs in the gravel beds of river bottoms by swishing her powerful tail. But what happens to all the fish when the rivers freeze up? Where do the fish go at 40 below?

"Fish in the Winter"

Young Readers:

Like all animals, fish know pretty well ahead of time when winter is coming. Before the water freezes, they swim away from the shallow creeks and rivers to the deep river sections or into deep lakes that don't freeze all the way to the bottom. Here they swim and wait until the winter is over. Some fish actually swim all the way to the ocean to get away from the freezing cold.

Advanced Readers:

In a strange twist of nature, spawned out salmon actually don't make it to the next winter. They all die within a few weeks of spawning. This makes a welcome meal for other animals, such as bears and eagles. Other fish species survive the winter just fine. Fish don't need to come up to the surface for breathing like the whales do because fish breathe through gills. Gills, in contrast to lungs, allow the fish to get oxygen directly from the water. So, as long as there is enough water, food and dissolved oxygen in the river or lake, it doesn't matter to the fish how much ice forms on top of the water. But, they better watch out what happens above the ice because some Alaskans love fishing so much that they also go fishing in the winter. How can they do that, you say? The fishermen cut holes in the ice through which they drop their fishing lines. This is called "ice-fishing."

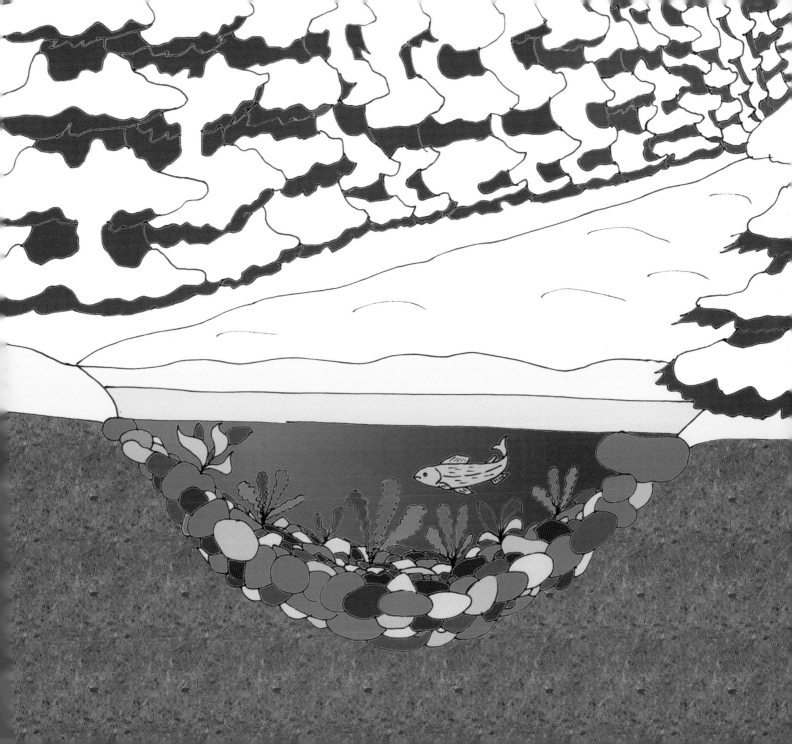

"Bear in the Summer"

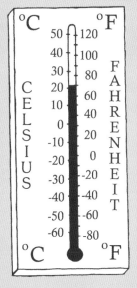

All Readers:

In Alaska, there are black bears, brown bears, and polar bears. They all are ferocious eaters. If they can catch another animal, they eat it. If they find a dead animal, they eat it. If they catch a fish, they eat it. They often walk for miles and miles just to find something to eat. On the way, the black and brown bears also stuff themselves with grasses and roots, and especially berries, which bears like very much. Actually, they don't just eat the berries - they eat the entire bush. You could say that bears will devour any food that will fit in their mouths and that they will eat 24 hours a day all summer long. Bears occasionally even break into cars and cabins if they detect the smell of food.

In the winter, berries and grasses don't grow and roots are covered by snow. There are no fish for bears because, as we already have learned, the rivers freeze. Hunting or finding dead animals becomes more difficult because of the ice and deep snow. So, what do hungry bears eat in the winter? Where do the bears go at 40 below?

"Bears in the Winter"

All Readers:

In the winter, bears don't go anywhere. Before the winter arrives, they look for or make themselves a cave, called a "den." If winter surprises them by coming early, they make a snow den. At the same time, bears get very sleepy. Once snow covers the land, they go into their dens and sleep through the entire winter. Sleeping through an entire winter is called "hibernation." During that time, bears don't eat or drink anything, which is why they ate so much the summer before. Can you see how big the sleeping bear is? It really must have eaten a lot last summer. Or could it be something else? If this is a female bear, maybe she is going to have little bear cubs. As strange as it may sound, bear cubs are born in the winter while the mother bears are hibernating.

Some areas in the southern part of Alaska don't get quite as cold as the rest of the state. There, bears may only hibernate a short time or not at all. Other animals that hibernate through the winter are the marmots, arctic ground squirrels, and chipmunks.

Summary

So, now we know where Alaska's animals go at 40 below. Do you remember which ones stay and live out in the cold? Were those the caribou, the moose, and the ptarmigan? Do you remember which ones hibernate through the winter? Could those have been the bears, arctic ground squirrels, marmots, and chipmunks? And which ones migrated to far-away places? Were the whales and Canada geese among them?

Where do animals go during the winter where you live? Do some of them hibernate or migrate? If so, which ones hibernate and which ones migrate?

Hey, we have an idea! Wouldn't it be great to write a story about the animals in your area, listing what they do and where they go during the winter, just like this book does? Give it a try. It will be fun!